Potato Clocks

and Solar Cars

Elizabeth Raum

www.raintreepublishers.co.uk
Visit our website to find out more information about Raintree books.

To order:
☎ Phone 44 (0) 1865 888112
📄 Send a fax to 44 (0) 1865 314091
💻 Visit the Raintree Bookshop at www.raintreepublishers.co.uk to browse our catalogue and order online.

First published in Great Britain by Raintree,
Halley Court, Jordan Hill, Oxford OX2 8EJ,
part of Harcourt Education.

Raintree is a registered trademark of Harcourt Education Ltd.

© Harcourt Education Ltd 2008
First published in paperback 2008
The moral right of the proprietor has been asserted.

Editorial: Nancy Dickmann and Catherine Veitch
Design: Philippa Jenkins
Illustrations: Peter Geissler
Picture Research: Hannah Taylor
Production: Alison Parsons

Originated by Modern Age
Printed and bound in China by Leo Paper Group

ISBN 978 1 4062 0740 8 (hardback)
12 11 10 09 08
10 9 8 7 6 5 4 3 2 1

ISBN 978 1 4062 0754 5 (paperback)
12 11 10 09 08
10 9 8 7 6 5 4 3 2 1

British Library Cataloguing in Publication Data
Raum, Elizabeth
Potato clocks and solar cars. – (Fusion)
333.7'94
A full catalogue record for this book is available from the British Library

Acknowledgements
The author and publisher are grateful to the following for permission to reproduce copyright material: Alamy Images/AA World Travel Library p.**25** inset; Alamy Images/David R. Frazier Photolibrary, Inc. p.**15**; Corbis pp.**6-7** (Ed Kashl), **19** (Reuters), **22-23** (Ron Watts), **11** (San Francisco Chronicle/ Michael Maloney), **16-17** (Walter Geiersperger); Empics/AP p.**21** inset; Getty Images/Stone pp.**20-21**, **24-25**, **28**; Getty Images/The Image Bank pp.**12-13**; Photolibrary pp.**8-9** (Martyn Chillmaid); Photolibrary/Index Stock Imagery pp.**4-5**, **10**; Reuters p.**14** (Toru Hanai); Rex Features p.**7** inset (Bulent Tavli); Still Pictures pp.**26-27** (Markus Dlouhy).

Cover photograph of potato clock reproduced with permission of Getty Images/Stone.

The publishers would like to thank Nancy Harris and Harold Pratt for their assistance with the preparation of this book.

Disclaimer
All the Internet addresses (URLs) given in this book were valid at the time of going to press. However, due to the dynamic nature of the Internet, some addresses may have changed, or sites may have changed or ceased to exist since publication. While the author and publishers regret any inconvenience this may cause readers, no responsibility for any such changes can be accepted by either the author or the publishers.

It is recommended that adults supervise children on the Internet.

Contents

Some words are printed in bold, **like this**. You can find out what they mean on page 30. You can also look in the box at the bottom of the page where they first appear.

Everyday energy

We use **energy** every day. Energy is the ability to make things move or change. We use energy for work and for fun. Energy lights, heats, and cools our homes. We use energy to run cars, lorries, and buses.

Hospitals count on energy every day. They use it to look after ill people. Office buildings and schools need energy, too.

Energy adds fun to our daily lives. Energy runs our televisions and computers. Without energy, we would not have films. Without energy, our lives would change in many ways. We depend on energy. But where does energy come from?

This computer needs energy to run.

energy ability to make things move or change

Dinosaur bones and dead plants

Much of the world's **energy** comes from one source. It comes from **fossil fuels**. Fossil fuels are made from dead animals and plants buried deep in the ground. Fossil fuels form over millions of years.

Coal is one type of fossil fuel. Coal is a rock. It is found all over the world. People use coal to heat houses and run factories.

Most cars use fossil fuels. ↓

coal   rock that gives energy when burned
fossil fuel   coal, oil, and natural gas
natural gas   underground gas that gives energy when burned
petroleum   oil that gives energy when burned

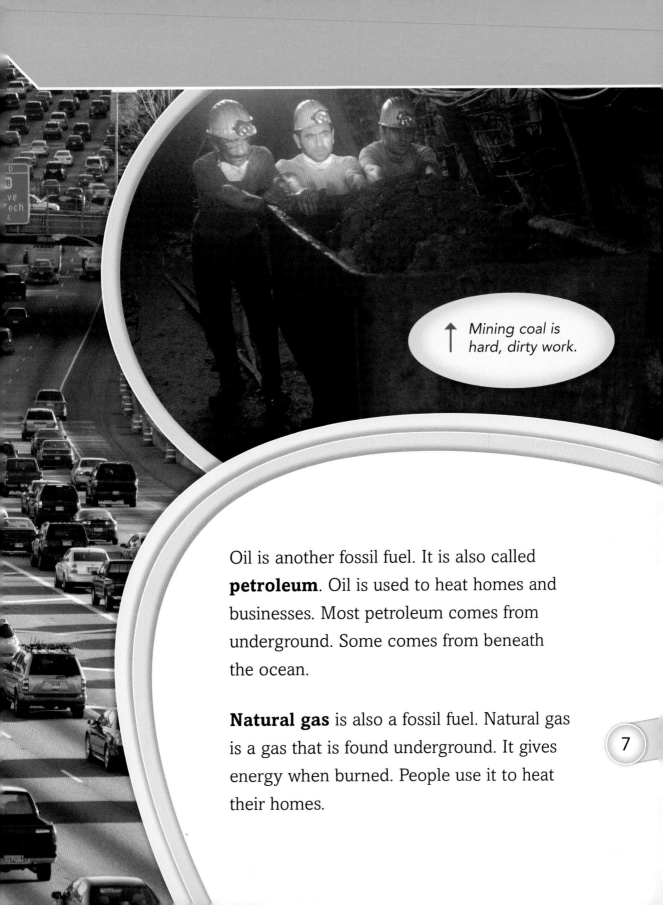

↑ *Mining coal is hard, dirty work.*

Oil is another fossil fuel. It is also called **petroleum**. Oil is used to heat homes and businesses. Most petroleum comes from underground. Some comes from beneath the ocean.

Natural gas is also a fossil fuel. Natural gas is a gas that is found underground. It gives energy when burned. People use it to heat their homes.

Potato clocks

No one knows how much longer **fossil fuels** will last. They are called **non-renewable energy** sources. This means we could use them up.

More and more people need energy. We must find sources that will not run out. We need to find new or **alternative** energy sources. These sources must be **renewable**. That means they will not run out.

The wind is renewable. It never runs out. Water is renewable, too. It replaces itself over time. So do potatoes!

Fossil fuels **pollute** the air, or make it dirty. This can make people ill.

	yes	no
Fossil fuels		
Renewable		✓
Clean		✓
Safe	✓*	
Low cost		✓

*Note: Although fossil fuels are normally safe to use, they can sometimes cause fires.

alternative new or different
non-renewable something that will not last forever
pollute make dirty or make unclean
renewable something that can be replaced over time

Creative clocks

Science students can use something special to run calculators and clocks. They use potatoes and lemons. Using potatoes and lemons for energy is fun. But their energy is very weak. It cannot heat a house or run a car.

This is a potato clock. It runs on energy made from metal and potato.

Pedalling a milkshake

People make **energy**, too. People can **renew** (replace)
their energy with a good meal and a nap. There are many
tasks we can do ourselves. We can wash dishes by hand.
We can hang washing outside to dry. Are there other ways
we can use our own energy?

Walking can take us to the tops of mountains. Walking can
take us to school or to the shops. Walking or cycling are
good ways to travel short distances.

*There are some
places you can only
reach on foot.*

This student uses bicycle pedals to run a blender. The pedals supply the energy to make it run.

People energy	yes	no
Renewable	✓	
Clean	✓	
Safe	✓	
Low cost	✓	

Note: Travel by foot or bike is slow and takes time.

Walk talk

A woman's average walking speed is 4.8 kilometres per hour (3 miles per hour). A man's is 5.6 kilometres per hour (3.5 miles per hour).

Energy from people works well for some things. But people energy cannot heat a home. People energy cannot run a factory. For those jobs, we need stronger energy.

Nuclear energy

The tiny parts that make up all things are called **atoms**. Splitting atoms into pieces makes **energy**. It is called **nuclear energy**.

Nuclear energy is powerful. It is made in a nuclear **power station**. It costs a lot to set up a nuclear power station. Electricity is made in a nuclear power station. Electricity is a type of energy. Electricity is used to power homes. It also powers offices and schools.

Nuclear energy	yes	no
Renewable		✓
Clean	✓*	
Safe		✓
Low cost	✓*	

*Notes: Nuclear energy makes waste that can pollute. It also costs a lot to set up a nuclear power station. Once it is set up, the energy costs very little.

This is a nuclear power station. Electricity is made here.

atom	tiny part that makes up all things
nuclear energy	energy made by splitting atoms
power station	factory that makes energy

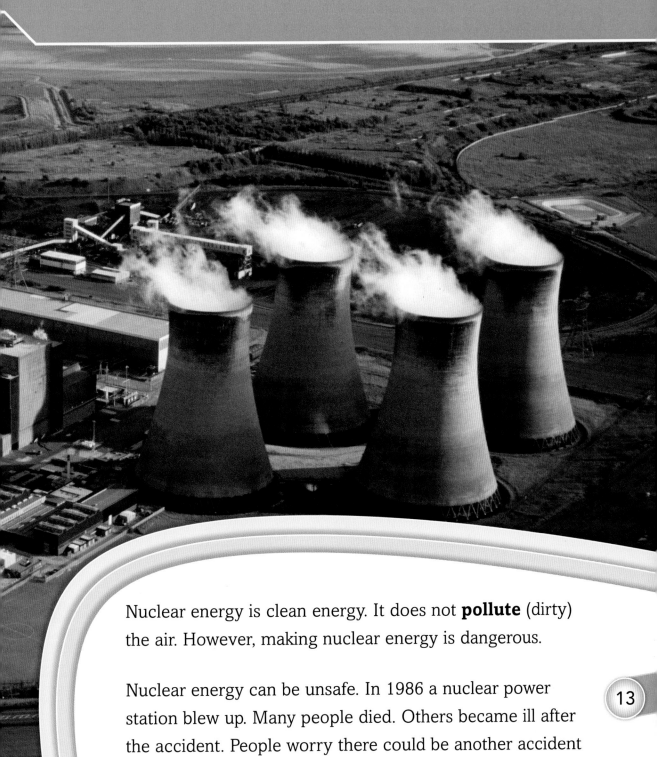

Nuclear energy is clean energy. It does not **pollute** (dirty) the air. However, making nuclear energy is dangerous.

Nuclear energy can be unsafe. In 1986 a nuclear power station blew up. Many people died. Others became ill after the accident. People worry there could be another accident at a nuclear power station. People are looking for safer sources of energy.

Soaking up rays

The Sun makes **energy**. It is called **solar energy**. It is clean and **renewable**. It never runs out. Solar energy is good in places where the Sun shines brightly. It is harder to get in places where trees and mountains block the Sun.

Solar panels are flat pieces of glass and other materials. They draw heat from the Sun. Solar cars use these panels to provide energy. Homes use solar panels for heat and hot water. The bigger the solar panels, the more energy they produce.

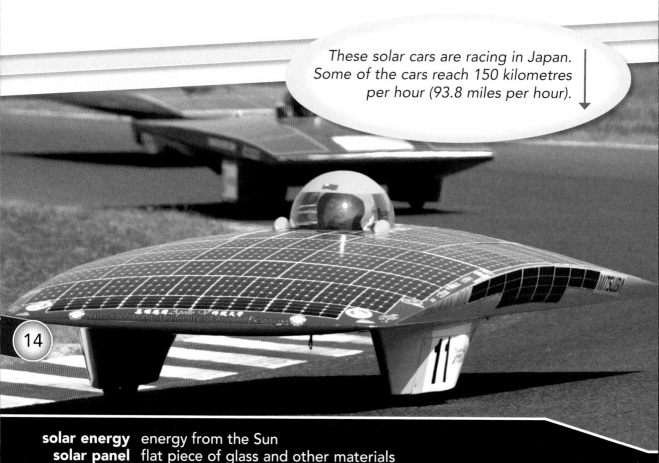

These solar cars are racing in Japan. Some of the cars reach 150 kilometres per hour (93.8 miles per hour).

solar energy   energy from the Sun
solar panel   flat piece of glass and other materials that trap energy from the Sun

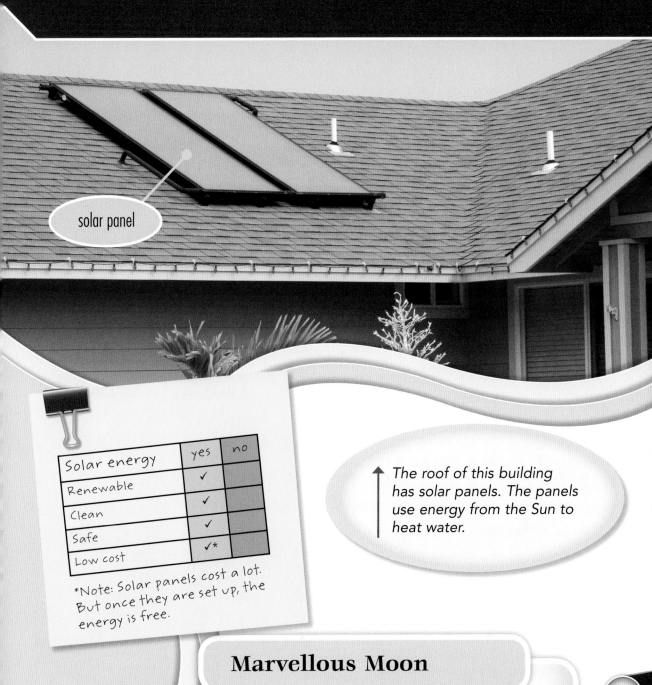

solar panel

Solar energy	yes	no
Renewable	✓	
Clean	✓	
Safe	✓	
Low cost	✓*	

*Note: Solar panels cost a lot. But once they are set up, the energy is free.

↑ *The roof of this building has solar panels. The panels use energy from the Sun to heat water.*

Marvellous Moon

In the future, we may build solar panels on the Moon. They could send solar energy to Earth.

Blowing in the wind

Wind is a **renewable energy** source. It never runs out. People built windmills hundreds of years ago. They used wind to pump water. Today, large windmills are called **wind turbines**. They turn wind energy into electricity. Electricity is a type of energy. Wind is the fastest-growing energy source in the world.

Wind farms may have hundreds of wind turbines.

Windy tale

In 2004 Dirk Gion travelled 2,976 kilometres (1,850 miles) on a skateboard. A giant sail used wind energy to push him along.

wind farm large group of wind turbines
wind turbine giant spinning blades on a tall tower used to gather wind energy

Wind does not blow all of the time. People who use wind energy need another source for calm days. In the future, large **wind farms** will store energy to use later.

Wind energy is not perfect. Wind farms take up a lot of space. The space could be used for farms or houses. Some people think wind turbines are ugly. Others worry that big wind turbines may kill birds.

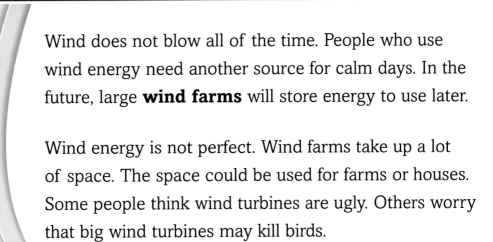

Wind	yes	no
Renewable	✓	
Clean	✓	
Safe	✓	
Low cost	✓*	

*Note: It costs a lot to set up wind farms, but the wind is free.

wind turbine

Corn and cows

People also use **biomass energy**. Biomass energy comes from burning plants. It also comes from animal waste. In the past, people got most of their **energy** from burning wood. People still burn wood today.

People find new ways to use biomass energy every day. Many people have begun to use **ethanol** in their cars. Ethanol is made from corn, sugar beets, or sugar cane. It is a type of biomass energy. It costs less than **fossil fuels**. These are fuels made from dead animals and plants. But biomass energy makes the air dirty. Fossil fuels also make the air dirty.

Trees and plants are **renewable** energy sources. They will not run out. However, it takes time and land to grow more trees.

Burn it!

About 2.5 billion people use biomass energy for cooking. They also use it for heating and lighting their homes.

biomass energy energy from burning plant or animal waste
ethanol type of fuel made from plants

Biomass	yes	no
Renewable	✓	
Clean		✓
Safe	✓	
Low cost	✓*	

*Note: Sometimes land needed for growing food is used for fuel instead.

Some fuel stations sell ethanol.

Cows can provide biomass energy to many homes in farming areas.

Helpful hens!

Farmers in the United Kingdom sell the wood chips they use to line chicken cages. They sell them to a power plant in Thetford. The plant turns the chips and other waste into gas. It provides biomass energy to 70,000 homes.

Cow energy

Cows and other animals provide a form of **biomass energy**. For hundreds of years, people burned animal waste for fuel. Animal waste is a form of biomass energy. Like all biomass energy, it is **renewable**. It can be made over and over again.

People still use **energy** from animals. In some places, animal waste is turned into gas. This gas is used for cooking and heating houses.

It is also possible to burn waste, or rubbish, to make gas. Many countries are looking into making fuel out of rubbish.

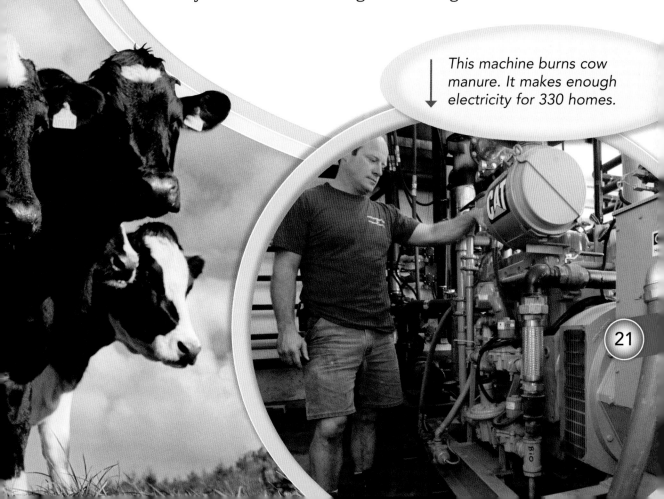

This machine burns cow manure. It makes enough electricity for 330 homes.

Water power

We can also get **energy** from falling water. This is called **hydroelectric energy**. Today, almost 25 per cent of the world's energy is hydroelectric.

The first step in making hydroelectric power is to stop water. You need to stop the flow of a river. A dam is built across the river. The dam holds back the water. The water behind the dam is called a **reservoir**. A **power station** is built at the bottom of the dam. Electricity is made in a power station. The dam is opened. The water rushes out. It passes through the power station and makes electricity.

Hydroelectric energy is **renewable**. It can be replaced. It does not **pollute** (dirty) the air. But it is costly to build a hydroelectric power station.

This is a photo of Niagara Falls in New York State, USA. One of the first hydroelectric stations was built here.

hydroelectric energy energy from falling water
reservoir large lake where water collects

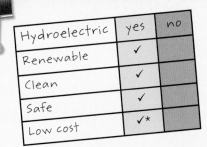

Hydroelectric	yes	no
Renewable	✓	
Clean	✓	
Safe	✓	
Low cost	✓*	

*Note: Power stations are costly, but the energy is not.

Niagara Falls

Ocean energy

Some people get **energy** from the ocean. It comes from the **tides**. Tides are the rising and falling of the surface of the ocean. **Tidal energy** is clean. It is **renewable**. It can be replaced.

Surfers use wave energy.

That's a lot of water!

About 70 per cent of Earth's surface is covered with water. That is a lot of waves!

tidal energy energy from ocean tides
tide rise and fall of the surface of the ocean

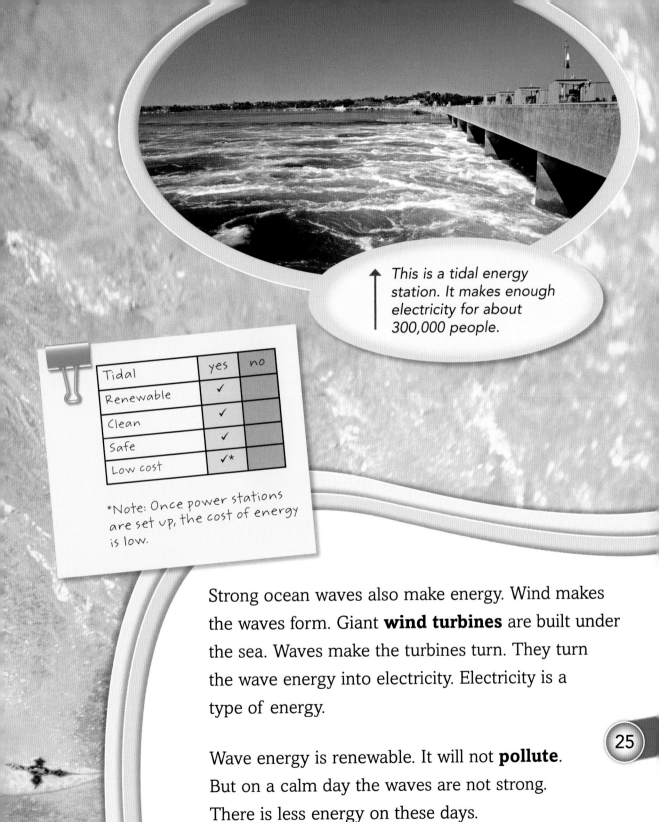

This is a tidal energy station. It makes enough electricity for about 300,000 people.

Tidal	yes	no
Renewable	✓	
Clean	✓	
Safe	✓	
Low cost	✓*	

*Note: Once power stations are set up, the cost of energy is low.

Strong ocean waves also make energy. Wind makes the waves form. Giant **wind turbines** are built under the sea. Waves make the turbines turn. They turn the wave energy into electricity. Electricity is a type of energy.

Wave energy is renewable. It will not **pollute**. But on a calm day the waves are not strong. There is less energy on these days.

Geothermal energy

In some places on Earth, hot water bubbles to the surface. This happens in lakes and streams. Heat makes the lake and stream water warm. This heat can be used to make **energy**. This energy is called **geothermal energy**. Geothermal energy comes from heat inside the Earth.

Geothermal energy is made in geothermal **power stations**. A power station is a factory that makes energy. Geothermal power stations are built in special places. They are near places where hot water comes to Earth's surface. They are by lakes or streams.

Most geothermal energy is used to make electricity.

Geothermal	yes	no
Renewable		✓
Clean	✓	
Safe	✓	
Low cost	✓*	

*Note: Once power stations are set up, the cost of energy is low.

geothermal energy energy that comes from heat inside Earth

Swimmers enjoy swimming in this hot water lake. The water is warm because of heat that comes from inside Earth. A geothermal power station uses the hot water to make electricity.

More and better energy

Energy comes from many different sources. It comes from **fossil fuels** and ourselves. It comes from **atoms** (tiny parts). It comes from the Sun and the wind. It comes from animal waste, water, and heat inside the Earth. Each energy source has good points and bad points.

Scientists will keep looking for **alternative** (new) energy sources. They will keep studying ways to make the energy sources we use today even better.

This photo of Earth at night was taken from space. Bright lights show the areas of greatest energy use. Find your home area. Is it well lit?

Energy	Renewable	Clean	Safe	Low cost	Notes
Fossil Fuels	✗	✗	✓*	✗	*Mining and oil drilling are dangerous. Fossil fuels can cause fires.
People	✓	✓	✓	✓	Travel by foot or bike is slow and takes time.
Nuclear	✗	✓	✗	✓*	*It costs a lot to set up a nuclear power station. Once it is set up, the energy costs very little.
Solar	✓	✓	✓	✓*	*Once solar panels are set up, the cost of energy is low. Panels take up lots of room.
Wind	✓	✓	✓	✓*	*It costs a lot to set up wind farms, but the wind is free. Wind farms need space. Some days there is no wind.
Biomass	✓	✗	✓	✓	Sometimes land needed for growing food is used for fuel instead.
Hydroelectric	✓	✓	✓	✓*	*Once power stations are set up, the cost of energy is low. Does not exist everywhere.
Tidal	✓	✓	✓	✓	Tidal energy only lasts ten hours a day.
Geothermal	✗	✓	✓	✓	Once power stations are set up, the cost of energy is low. Does not exist everywhere.

Glossary

alternative new or different. Solar energy is an alternative energy source.

atom tiny part that makes up all things. Everything you see around you is made up of atoms.

biomass energy energy from burning plant or animal waste

coal rock that gives energy when burned. Digging for coal is dangerous.

energy ability to make things move or change. We use energy every day.

ethanol type of fuel made from plants. Some petrol stations sell ethanol.

fossil fuel coal, oil, and natural gas. Fossil fuels pollute and are non-renewable.

geothermal energy energy that comes from heat inside Earth. Geothermal power stations are often near warm lakes.

hydroelectric energy energy from falling water. Many waterfalls supply hydroelectric energy.

natural gas underground gas that gives energy when burned. Natural gas is used to run some ovens.

non-renewable something that will not last forever. Oil is non-renewable.

nuclear energy energy made by splitting atoms. Nuclear energy is very powerful.

petroleum oil that gives energy when burned. Most cars use petroleum.

pollute make dirty or make unclean. Solar energy does not pollute the air.

power station factory that makes energy

renewable something that can be replaced over time. Rain shows us that water is renewable.

reservoir large lake where water collects

solar energy energy from the Sun. Many people in poor countries use solar energy to run small ovens.

solar panel flat piece of glass and other materials that trap energy from the Sun. Some calculators run on tiny solar panels.

tidal energy energy from ocean tides. Tidal energy is fun for surfers.

tide rise and fall of the surface of the ocean. Usually the tide rises and falls twice every 24 hours.

wind farm large group of wind turbines. Wind farms take up a lot of land.

wind turbine giant spinning blades on a tall tower used to gather wind energy. Some people say wind turbines are noisy and ugly.

Want to know more?

Books to read

- *Looking at Energy: Wind Power*, Polly Goodman (Hodder Wayland, 2005)

- *Fantastic Forces: Gravity*, Chris Oxlade (Heinemann Library, 2007)

- *A True Book: Solar Power*, Christine Petersen (Children's Press, 2004)

- *Fantastic Forces: Speed and Acceleration*, Richard Spilsbury (Heinemann Library, 2007)

Websites

- www.sciencemuseum.org.uk/exhibitions/energy/site/quiz3.asp
  Find out more about energy in the future.
- www.nef.org.uk/powered/documents/RenewableEnergy.pdf
  Learn more about renewable energy.

To find out how energy can be used in all kinds of weird and wonderful ways, read ***Wackiest Machines Ever!***

Go on a search and rescue mission to find a missing commando. Learn all about the different energy you will use on your trip in ***Search and Rescue***.

Index